Co-Published by

**GENERAL STORE**
**PUBLISHING HOUSE**

499 O'Brien Road, Box 415, Renfrew, Ontario, Canada K7V 4A6
Telephone: (613) 432-7697 or 1-800-465-6072
**www.gsph.com**

with

Maxi Publishing
Ashton, Ontario K0A 1B0

ISBN 1-897113-21-8

Printed and bound in Canada

Design, layout and printing by Custom Printers of Renfrew Ltd.

Text and illustration copyright ©2004 Lesley Anne Airth

**Library and Archives Canada Cataloguing in Publication Data**

Airth, Lesley Anne
What we remember / Lesley Anne Airth ; Mervyn Finch, illustrator.

ISBN 1-897113-21-8

1. Canada--History, Military--Juvenile literature.  2. War--Juvenile literature.  3. Remembrance Day (Canada)--Juvenile literature.
        I. Finch, Mervyn  II. Title.

D680.C2A37 2005          971        C2005-903301-0

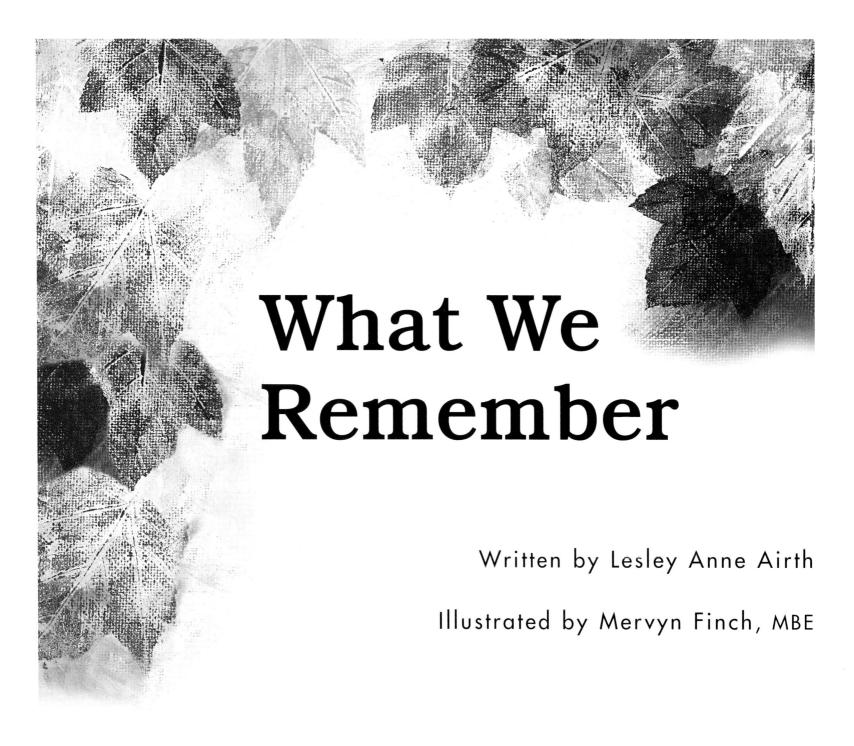

# What We Remember

Written by Lesley Anne Airth

Illustrated by Mervyn Finch, MBE

*This book is dedicated to the
brave Canadian men and women
who risked all in the cause
of freedom.*

# Introduction

"Wait for Me, Daddy"

"Wait for Me, Daddy", by Claude Detloff, was taken on October 1, 1940. It soon became one of the most popular pictures of its time, and it's easy to see why. In one poignant image Claude Detloff portrayed the sheer numbers of brave Canadians who volunteered to serve overseas, and the fact that the costs of war would also be borne by families … including young children.

Millions of Canadians have been affected by the tragedy of war. It is a horrendous subject and one that is not normally shared with children. However, I believe that children – even young children – should understand how fortunate we are to live in a peaceful society, and how grateful we ought to be to those who fought for our freedom. There is no question that these are difficult lessons to teach, yet we must. To do so, we need be aware of children's sensibilities and share stories that do not frighten or overwhelm them.

The stories in *What We Remember* are based on the actual experiences of real people. Thousands of Canadians have had similar experiences. It is my hope that sharing these stories will foster a sense of pride in our Canadian heritage, spark an interest in history and, above all, nurture an appreciation of the sacrifices made by so many men and women so that we and others can live in peace.

*Lesley Anne Airth*

# ❧ The Ship ❧

J ohn was fast asleep when suddenly ... THUMP ... the ship shook so hard he nearly fell out of his bunk. Alarm bells began ringing. People started running and yelling outside his cabin door. It seemed like a bad dream – but he wasn't dreaming! John knew instantly that something terrible had happened, and he soon discovered that an enemy torpedo had blasted a hole in the side of the ship. In the middle of the Atlantic Ocean on a cold, black night, John was about to have the most dangerous adventure of his life.

When the Second World War started, John was a 12-year-old schoolboy living in England. At first, the war had seemed far away and not very frightening. But it wasn't long before enemy planes started dropping bombs. Night after night, the bombs fell on cities and towns in England. People had to go to bomb shelters in special underground hideaways so that they wouldn't be hurt. It was very frightening.

Afraid that something terrible would happen to their son, John's parents decided to send him to a boarding school in Canada. They knew that John would be safer once he arrived in Canada, but they were very worried about the dangerous voyage across the Atlantic Ocean.

 "Don't tell anyone about your trip to Canada," his parents had warned. "Don't even tell your best friends at school. This trip must be kept secret!"

He wanted to talk about his trip, but John knew that during the war nobody ever talked about when or where ships were sailing. Enemy submarines had sunk many ships. If the enemy discovered when or where a ship was travelling, that ship would be an easy target.

John's ship set sail from Liverpool. He was traveling with a chaperone – a nice lady who'd been asked to look after him on the trip. He discovered that there were hundreds of children on board the big ship – some with their mothers and some with chaperones. Like him, they were all being sent away to escape the bombings.

As the ship sailed slowly down the river toward the ocean, John was too excited to stay in his cabin. He stood on the deck in the cold rain so that he wouldn't miss anything. He'd been told that the trip would be dangerous, but he wasn't afraid until he began seeing sunken ships along the river. His whole body tingled with fear when he saw one sunken ship with just the tip of the mast sticking out of the water.

On the first morning of their trip, John and his chaperone had practised putting on lifejackets and getting into the lifeboat that had been assigned to them. They had to practise – just in case there was an emergency.

And now, the loud clanging of alarm bells outside his door told John that there was an emergency!

Suddenly, the door to his cabin flew open and in rushed his chaperone.

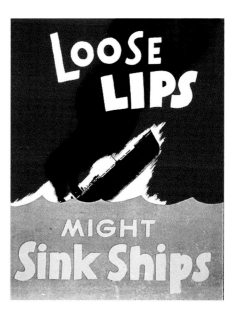

*John Hassell was born in England. In 1940, when he was 12 years old, he was sent to Canada to attend Albert College in Belleville, Ontario. John and his wife Mora are retired and live on Vancouver Island, British Columbia.*

"Hurry, John!" she exclaimed. "We have to get into the lifeboat right away."

John grabbed his slippers and his red housecoat – there wasn't time for anything else. Together, they rushed to the deck. They both knew that the ship might sink quickly!

It was after midnight, but the bright lights all over the deck made it easy to see where they were going. Everyone quickly put on lifejackets and climbed into the lifeboats. As the small lifeboat was cautiously lowered to the ocean, the ship's lights dimmed and then went out. John peered over the edge of the lifeboat. All he could see was the eerie blackness of the water below. When the lifeboat finally touched down on the ocean, John could hear the voices of people in other lifeboats. He listened to the sounds, but he couldn't see anything in the darkness that surrounded them.

A man seated near John shouted, "Quickly! Row! We have to move away from the ship!"

Everyone tried to work quickly, but most of the people in the lifeboat didn't know how to row. Nobody had practised rowing. Some people rowed forward and some rowed backward. They weren't getting anywhere until an older gentleman started giving instructions. He'd been a sea captain and he showed some of the adults how to hold the oars and which way to pull them.

As they slowly and steadily moved away from the side of the damaged vessel, John and the others looked back. What a frightening sight! John's heart raced; he could feel the pounding in his chest. There was just enough moonlight to see the outline of the crippled hulk. The once great ship that had moved so quickly through the water was sitting motionless, tipped to one side and helpless.

The icy ocean spray stung John's cheeks. Everybody was frightfully cold. The lifeboat rocked in the heavy swell of the ocean and made John and many others feel seasick.

The lifeboat drifted for several hours – it seemed ever so tiny on the vast, black ocean. They were far out at sea and no land could be seen anywhere. Everyone huddled together to try to stay warm. John wondered how many days they'd have to wait before they'd be found ... he even wondered if they'd ever be found.

Then, just before the sun came up, a navy tanker ship arrived. All of the people in the lifeboat cheered because they knew they were going to be rescued. The tanker was small – it was the kind of ship that was used to deliver fresh water to the big ships during the war. There were only twenty sailors on board, but they all worked quickly. They helped everyone in John's lifeboat climb onto the tanker.

As soon as everyone was safe, the little tanker started searching for other lifeboats. By dawn, they had rescued over a hundred people. Everyone was given a warm place to sleep, a cup of tea and a biscuit. The biscuit was so hard it nearly broke John's teeth. The sailors slept out on the cold steel deck because there was no place for them inside.

After a day of sailing, the little rescue ship carried them all safely into harbour at Glasgow, Scotland. The very next day, John went back to his boarding school in England. His parents were happy he was safe, but once again they began making secret plans to send him to Canada.

Only a few weeks later, John and his chaperone sailed from Liverpool on another big ship. They were both very nervous because they didn't want another dangerous adventure! Fortunately, John and all of the other passengers were lucky. They crossed the Atlantic safely, and John wasn't even seasick. John and his parents were relieved and happy when he reached the safety of Canada!

## Tulips

During World War II, the future queen of the Netherlands, Princess Juliana, and her young daughters lived safely in Ottawa while Canadians were fighting to liberate their homeland. At the end of the war, Princess Juliana and the Dutch people wanted to say thank you to all Canadians for their help and friendship during the war. Not only did they want to thank Canada for allowing the Dutch Royal family to come and live safely in Ottawa, but they wanted to remember the thousands of Canadians who fought and died liberating their country. As a lasting symbol of friendship, they have been sending thousands of tulip bulbs to Ottawa every year since 1945. Each spring, in Canada's Capital Region, more than 1 million tulips bloom in front of the Parliament Buildings and in public parks.

## Discussion Questions

1. Why did people in England want to send their children away?

2. Was John safe when he left England?

# ❧ The Medal ❧

**S**hortly after the First World War, on a cold winter morning in northern Ontario, Malcolm awoke and heard the sound of laughter outside his house. He jumped out of his cozy bed and used his fingernails to scrape off the thick coat of frost from the bedroom window. There on the pond – just behind the shed – his friends were already playing hockey! He quickly pulled his favourite white sweater over his head, buttoned up his breeches and raced down to the kitchen.

When Malcolm went into the bright, sunny kitchen he could feel the warmth from the big wood stove. His stomach rumbled with hunger as he smelled the delicious oatmeal bubbling on the burner.

"Breakfast's almost ready," his mom said, as she gave him a hug. "While I finish cooking your porridge, will you carry these boxes to the basement, please?"

"O.K.," he said cheerfully – even though he could hardly wait to get outside with his friends.

He was only eight, but Malcolm always helped his mom around the house. He carried in the wood for the wood stove, swept the floors and made the beds. His father was often too weak and sick to work. His dad had been that way ever since he'd come back from fighting in the war.

Malcolm was in a hurry to carry the boxes downstairs. He knew he was already late for the backyard hockey game. He piled the boxes in a tall stack, but when he reached the top of the stairs, the stack started to tip. CRASH! BANG! CRASH! All the boxes tumbled down the stairs. Lids and boxes and papers and photographs were scattered all over the basement floor.

"Oops! Sorry, Mom," he said as he looked down at the big mess.

"I'll help you pick everything up," sighed his mother, "But next time, try to be more careful. Make two or three trips."

When he reached the bottom of the stairs, Malcolm noticed a shiny silver cross attached to a white and purple ribbon sticking out from under a pile of papers. He picked it up and the little piece of metal felt cold in his hand.

"What's this?" he asked, holding it up for his mom to see.

"It's a medal. It was given to your father during the war," she answered.

"What's a medal?" asked Malcolm as he ran his fingers over the little crowns on the corners of the cross.

"It's a very special award," said his mom. "People who've shown bravery or have served their country in an important way are awarded medals. There are different kinds of medals, and each one has its own special meaning."

"What kind is this?"

"It's called the Military Cross and it's given to soldiers who've done something particularly brave," she explained. "They said your father showed 'splendid courage and determination' when they awarded him this medal. He was a hero."

Malcolm could hardly believe his ears! He couldn't imagine that his father was a hero. He couldn't run, or even walk very far. Most of the time, he had to sit quietly and rest because he found it hard to breathe. "But … but, he's so weak," said Malcolm. "How could he be a hero?"

With a sad look on her face, Malcolm's mom stopped picking up the mess and sat down beside him on the rough wooden step. "He wasn't always weak," she said as her voice trembled and her eyes filled with tears. "Before the Great War, he was a strong, healthy man. Like so many thousands of brave men who fought in the war, he wasn't strong and healthy when he returned home."

Malcolm felt very sad when he saw his mom crying. "Will he ever get better?" he asked hopefully.

His mom shook her head and said, "He'll never be as healthy as he was before the war," – she paused a long moment before adding with a soft smile – "but we're so lucky to have him home with us."

Malcolm Airth, pictured with his grandfather and sister Ailsa, was born in Renfrew County, Ontario, in 1922. As an adult, he served in the Royal Canadian Air Force during the Second World War.

## The Great War 1914-1918

The First World War was called the Great War because it was the biggest war there had ever been. Only 8 million people lived in Canada in 1914, but 628,462 Canadians enrolled in the military and 424,589 went overseas to fight. 60,661 Canadians died. The Great War was also called "the War to end all Wars" because everyone thought it would be the last war ever.

Malcolm knew he was very lucky that his dad had come home from the war. He knew that many fathers hadn't returned. Their names were on the stone monument in the town park.

"What did Dad do that was so brave?" asked Malcolm as he slowly turned the silver medal over in his hand and looked at it closely.

"Just going off to war takes great courage," said his mother, "but your dad did something especially brave in a place called Passchendaele. He was in an awful battle there, and many, many Canadians were killed. In the middle of the fighting he was asked to get some important information. The only way to get it was to cross an open field in front of enemy soldiers. It was scary and very dangerous. But your dad said he would try to do it. He crossed that field even though it was still daylight and there was no place to hide from the gunfire."

Malcolm's heart thumped and he shivered with fear. He quickly asked, "Did Dad get the information?"

"Yes," said his mom, "But it took him a long time to cross that muddy field. It was November and the weather was wet and cold. He had to wade through deep, thick mud that was nearly up to his waist. After that terrible day, he became very sick and hasn't been able to get better. Your dad will never again be a strong man," she said quietly, "But, he'll always be a hero."

Malcolm had forgotten about going outside to play hockey with his friends. He just sat quietly beside his mom on the basement stairs and thought about the medal and about his dad. He was so proud that his dad was a hero.

## Passchendaele

Passchendaele was a lovely little village in Belgium in 1914. Four years later, when the war ended, every building and every tree had been destroyed. There was nothing left but a sea of mud. The village had disappeared. Many Canadian heroes helped win the Battle of Passchendaele but, sadly, there were nearly 16,000 casualties.

11

After a while, he turned to his mom and asked if they could take the medal upstairs and put it in a special place.

"That's a wonderful idea," she replied.

Malcolm started up the stairs, holding the medal with both hands. This time he wanted to be very, very careful.

*John McIntyre Airth, Malcolm's father, served in the 3rd Battalion, Canadian Expeditionary Force during the First World War. He fought in two of that war's most famous and tragic battles, Vimy Ridge and Passchendaele.*

## Discussion Questions

1. Why was the First World War called the Great War?

2. World War I was also called the "War to end all Wars." Did it end all wars?

3. Why was Malcolm's father given a medal?

# ❧ The Photograph ❧

**B**ill's heart pounded with excitement as he looked at the calendar. "Just two more days until Saturday!" he said to himself. He was almost six years old, and this Saturday was going to be the best day of his life. Bill's dad was coming home from the war.

He ran to the living room to look at the photograph on the mantle. Bill had never known his dad, but his mother told him that the man in the picture was his father. The small black and white photograph had been on the mantle for as long as Bill could remember. His father was wearing a uniform, and he had a friendly smile on his face. It had always been Bill's favourite picture.

Whenever he looked at the photograph, Bill tried to imagine what it would be like to have his father in the house. He wondered if he and his dad would go skating and tobogganing together. Would his father help him make model trains? Would he read stories to him?

His mother and his aunt talked about his dad, but they weren't boys, and the man in the photograph wasn't their father! He didn't have any brothers or sisters to tell him about his dad.

His friends' fathers had gone away to war too. In fact, he didn't know any men his father's age – just older gentlemen who were too old to go to war and teenage boys who were still too young to go.

Every year on Bill's birthday, his aunts saved their sugar ration coupons so that his mom could make him a chocolate cake iced with thick marshmallow frosting. Every year, just before he blew out the candles on the cake, his mom asked him to make a wish. Every year, Bill made the same wish ... that the war would be over and his dad could come home.

One wonderful spring day, news came that the war in Europe was over. All the fathers and mothers who were serving overseas would be coming home. At last, Bill would get his wish! Everyone was excited. Especially Bill.

But the next days, weeks and months passed very slowly. Bill's dad didn't come home that summer like some of his friends' fathers. He didn't come home for Christmas that year either. Bill received letters from his dad telling him how much he missed him. His dad explained that he was helping people who'd been hurt by the war but that he'd be coming home as soon as he could.

When the letter came telling Bill that his dad would be home in just three weeks, he started counting days on the calendar. Now, there were only two days to go! He was too excited to go out and play with his friends. Instead, Bill stayed inside and helped his mom get ready for Saturday. They were having a party, and he wanted to

William Eugene Bawden was born in Toronto, Ontario. He served overseas for almost six years, returning to Canada in 1946. He continued to serve in the army until his retirement in 1961.

## Rationing

During the Second World War, gasoline and certain foods, such as sugar, were in short supply. A system of rationing was used to make sure that all Canadians could receive a fair share. Coupons had to be used to purchase rationed items.

help decorate the house with streamers and make a big "Welcome Home" sign for the front door.

Saturday finally arrived. Bill crept out of bed when it was still dark outside. He was more excited than he'd ever been ... even more excited than on Christmas morning! With great care, he put on his brand new shirt and pants. It took him a long time to get dressed because the collar on his new shirt was stiff, and it was hard to do up the top button.

When he was all dressed, he snuck quietly into the living room to look at the face in the photograph one more time. Then he went upstairs to wake up his mom, but she was already up and dressed – and almost as excited as Bill.

Bill and his mother and his aunt drove to a big arena in the centre of the city. When they went inside, Bill saw that there was no ice – only a dirt floor. The stands were filled with happy people who were cheering and clapping and waving little flags. It was so noisy, Bill could hardly hear what people were saying to him. He followed his mom and his aunt up the stairs and they found a good place to sit – they needed ten seats because Bill's great uncles and aunts were also coming. Everybody wanted to be at the homecoming.

Bill's mother explained that they would see hundreds of soldiers marching in a parade. Bill knew that his dad would be one of them.

Suddenly the band started to play. Soldiers began marching into the arena. The cheering was even louder! At first, Bill thought that the soldiers all looked the same – they all had khaki uniforms and big boots. Bill studied every face. He was certain he'd be the first one to spot his father. His mother didn't seem to think that was possible. But then it happened. He saw him. He knew it was him! Bill's heart was racing.

When he pointed out his father, Bill's mother seemed surprised ... then a huge smile lit up her face. But, only a moment later, she started to cry. Everyone seemed to be crying – even his great uncles had tears in their eyes. They all knew how lucky they were that Bill's dad was home safely from the war.

When the last soldiers finally marched into the arena the band stopped; then the parade stopped. The soldiers stood perfectly still – like statues. After a long pause, someone shouted something and suddenly the soldiers started moving about. Now all the soldiers looked happy – they began talking and laughing and shaking hands. Bill couldn't sit still any longer. He asked if he could go down to meet his father. He wanted to be first!

His mother, still crying, nodded yes, so Bill raced down the steps to the floor of the arena.

## The Home Front

At the beginning of the Second World War, Canada had a population of only 10 million people. Amazingly, nearly one million Canadians joined the military! With so many men away at war, the women left behind in Canada had to work very, very hard. They looked after the homes and farms and started doing jobs that had always been done by men. Women worked in shipyards, smelters and airplane factories. They also helped the men and women who were away at war by baking cookies, knitting warm woolen clothing and gathering newspapers to send overseas.

16

17

It was crowded and everyone else was twice as tall as Bill, but he remembered where he'd seen his dad and he headed for that spot. Sure enough, he found him standing in a circle of men. Bill stood silently and waited as the men talked. He was so nervous he felt as though butterflies were flying about in his stomach. The collar on his new shirt was hurting his neck, but he wouldn't open the button – he wanted to look perfect for his dad.

It seemed like he'd been standing there a long time when his father turned and saw him. Bill knew that his father recognized him – the same smile he knew from the photograph instantly appeared on his father's face.

"Hello Bill," said his father, and they shook hands.

"How do you do," replied Bill. A thrill of excitement suddenly ran through his body. "How did you know it was me?"

"I've a photograph of you here in my pocket," answered his dad, as he gently touched the pocket over his heart. "I've looked at pictures of you every day for almost six years, and I've watched you grow from a little baby to a big boy."

For a brief moment, they stood quietly in the middle of the crowded, noisy arena. They just looked at each other. Bill was so happy to be standing beside his father. Then his dad put his hand on Bill's shoulder and said, "I think it's time we all go home."

William (Bill) Bawden was born in Toronto, Ontario, in 1940. He joined the Canadian army and served for 36 years.

## Discussion Questions

1. When Bill was a young boy, did he know much about his father?

2. Why was a cake a special treat?

3. Why do you think that Bill was lucky?

18

# ❧ The Secret ❧

**T**he slender, dark haired lady glanced over her shoulder as she walked down the busy street. From time to time she stopped in front of a store window to look at the reflections of people behind her. The lady was Jacquie and John's mother, and she wanted to be sure that she wasn't being followed. What she was about to do was very important and quite dangerous!

When she arrived at the stately hotel, their mother checked again to be sure that no one was watching; then she stepped inside through a back door. She knew exactly where she was going, whom she had to meet, and what she had to do.

Only five minutes later, she left the hotel by another door and hurried down the street. The thick brown envelope she'd been given was safely hidden in her large bag. Now, she had to get to the airport as quickly as possible. She knew the envelope she was delivering contained information that could help win the war.

During the Second World War, Jacquie and John's mother was often asked to get important information. It was her job. It was a dangerous job, and she always had to be very careful that nobody suspected what she was doing. She was a secret agent!

Everything she did and everywhere she went had to be kept secret. She never told anyone about her work – not even her own family. Jacquie and John had no idea their mother was a spy. All they knew was that their family was not like other families.

When Jacquie was 8 and John was 6, they began to realize that their family was different. Whilst other children were sent away from England for their safety, Jacquie and John's mother took them *to* England. On a cold November day, they set sail from Halifax on a ship that was carrying guns and tanks. They were surrounded by navy ships for protection. No one could explain why the tiny, elegant lady and her two small children were on their way to England in the middle of the war. Even the sailors who were with them didn't know why they were making such a dangerous trip.

Shortly after they arrived in England, the children were sent to live in an old boarding school on the moors of Northern England. Their father was away at war, and they didn't want to leave their mother. But she explained that living in the countryside was not as dangerous as living in London. What their mother couldn't tell them was that she had secret assignments that had to be completed.

Jacquie and John's mother wasn't able to visit them very often. They missed their parents terribly as they lay in bed at night, listening to the wind howling through the trees outside and the mice scurrying under their beds. Every school holiday, they'd watch from their bedroom windows as cars would drive up the lane and stop to pick up children in front of the school.

## Spy Work

In wartime, it is important to have as much information as possible about your enemy. This is the work of spying. In all of Canada's wars, brave Canadian women and men have taken great risks in the secret world of spies. Their successes helped shorten wars and saved lives.

## Women Overseas

Women have served as nurses in all Canada's wars since 1885. Beginning in the Second World War, women were asked to perform many other important jobs in the military. During that war, in addition to nurses, nearly 5000 Canadian women served overseas. Women pilots delivered airplanes; others were radio operators, drivers, mechanics, secretaries and clerks.

They felt very lonely as they watched their friends going home for the holidays. Their mother was never there waiting to take them home – not even at Christmas.

It wasn't until many years after the war, when Jacquie and John were grown-ups, that they learned a little bit about their mother's work. They learned that while they were safe at school in the English countryside, their mother was doing dangerous work gathering important information that she hoped would help in the struggle to win the war.

Jacquie and John learned that their mother could speak several different languages, so if she were sent to far-off places to get information, she could travel in disguise. She spoke French, and if she traveled in France, she could pretend to be a French lady. She spoke Romanian and she could pretend to be a Romanian lady. On other occasions, she could be disguised as an Italian or a German lady.

They learned that while they had been lonely at school, their mother had been lonely too. Instead of being at home with her husband and two young children, she had been all alone, working far away from the people she loved. But their mother had known that if the war was going to end, she had to do what she could to help. She had worked day and night because she knew that every secret message she sent could offer a clue that might help end the war.

Jacquie and John learned that their mother's messages were sent by secret code. She was one of the very few people

Marion de Chastelain was an American who lived in Romania as a child and was educated in schools throughout Europe. During the Second World War she was a spy working first in New York with Sir William Stephenson ("The Man Called Intrepid") and later in Britain's Secret Intelligence Service.

Jacquie Brewster and John de Chastelain were born in Romania. When the de Chastelain family moved to Alberta in the 1950s they became Canadian citizens. Jacquie and her family live in Canmore, Alberta. John, who now lives in Ottawa, joined the Canadian Army and retired as Chief of the Defence Staff. He also served as Canada's Ambassador in Washington.

in the world who knew about a special code machine that had been invented by a Canadian.

During the war, Jacquie and John's mother had lots of secrets. In the many years since the end of the war, only a few of their mother's secrets have been revealed. However, what Jacquie and John do know is that their mother was clever and determined and brave. They will always be very proud of her.

## Rockex

During the Second World War, a brilliant Canadian professor from the University of Toronto invented a machine that could automatically change words into code or change code into words. This machine, called the Rockex, was extremely helpful for quickly sending and receiving messages that could not be understood by the enemy.

## Discussion Questions

1. Why were messages sent in code?

2. What roles did women play in the war effort?

# The Telegram

The news came on a warm spring day as Jean sat at her school desk. She could hear the excitement in the principal's deep voice as he said, "I have an announcement to make. It's the greatest announcement I could ever hope to make. The war in Europe is over! The war is finally over!"

Suddenly, there was shouting and cheering coming from all over the school. There was so much cheering and so much noise that they barely heard the principal announce that school was cancelled for the rest of the day. All of the students and teachers were allowed to go home to celebrate with their families.

At first, Jean didn't move – she just sat silently at her old wooden desk. Then, a moment later, she stood up and hurried out of the high school. As she ran down the steps toward the street, she saw people everywhere hugging and celebrating. The sound of cheering voices and honking horns was so loud, the noise was almost deafening. Everyone was happy. Everyone except Jean.

As she walked home alone, all Jean could think about was her dad. She remembered helping him fix the socks that he wore with his kilt. She remembered the parades in which her father had played the bagpipes and marched in the band. She remembered the thrill of tobogganing with her father and her little sister Mora as her mother and baby Jock looked on. She remembered spending hours in the garden working happily beside him. And ... she remembered the day that her dad went away forever.

It had been more than four years since her father had left for war, but Jean could never forget the day they said good-bye. Jock had been too young to understand, but Jean and Mora both knew that going to war meant great danger. On the morning their father went away, Jean had begged him not to go. "Why can't you stay home with us?" Jean asked. "You could get hurt if you go to war and it's safe in Canada."

Jean's father brushed away a tear from his cheek before he answered. "Let me try to explain why I have to go," he said, as he sat down beside Jean and put his strong arm around her shoulders. "I don't want to go away to war. Wars are horrible and frightening. And, more than anything, I don't want to leave your mother and you and Mora and Jock."

## Canada Wasn't Safe

During the Second World War enemy submarines came very close to Canada's shores. Many ships were sunk in Canadian waters. Canadians living close to coastal waters were trained to watch for and report sightings of enemy ships. At night all their windows had to be covered so that the enemy couldn't see them.

John MacNeil lived on Cape Breton Island when he joined the army to serve in the First World War. Too old to join the army in the Second World War, he nevertheless wanted to serve. He left his teaching post at Ottawa's Glebe Collegiate and joined the Royal Canadian Legion's Auxiliary as an education officer. On 30 April 1941, John MacNeil and many others died when their ship, the SS Nerissa, was sunk on its way to England.

"Then why are you going?" Jean blurted out as she started to cry.

"I'm going because innocent men, women and children are suffering," her father said, shaking his head sadly. There are people doing very bad things to others – they've started a war so that they can get things that don't belong to them. People who are not able to defend themselves are losing everything – their houses, their land and most importantly, their freedom.

"But the war is far away from us," Jean sobbed.

"It doesn't matter how far away the war is," her father said as he gave Jean a gentle hug. "People who do evil things and harm others must be stopped! We all have a duty to help those who aren't able to help themselves."

And then her father added, "It may seem as though we're safe in Canada because there aren't bombs exploding around us, but we're in danger too. If we don't stop these people, no one will be free."

Before he left, Jean's father had told her that he'd be sailing across the ocean on a large ship. He promised that as soon as he arrived in England he'd send her a letter to tell her about the trip. Jean never received a letter. Instead, only a short time after her father set sail, a telegram was delivered to her house, and Jean learned that her dad would never be coming home again. His ship had been sunk by enemy torpedoes. Her father and many other people on board had died.

## The Books of Remembrance

The names of 114,710 Canadian men and women who died in battle outside Canada are written on the pages of six beautiful books called *The Books of Remembrance*. These books are in a special room in the Peace Tower of Canada's Parliament buildings. Every day, there is a solemn ceremony to turn the pages of the books.

And now the war was over. Jean knew that thousands and thousands of fathers and mothers would soon be returning home to their families in Canada. She also knew that her father wouldn't be with them.

Jean was almost home from school when she stopped walking. She stood quietly, watching the people hugging and kissing and celebrating in the street. As she listened to the happy voices all around her, she began to realize that it was because of her father, and so many people like him, that the war was finally over.

Jean ran the rest of the way home. She knew that her family would celebrate the end of the fighting. They'd celebrate that people who'd lost their freedom were once again living in peace and that Canadians who'd helped win that freedom were coming home at last. And, on that special day, as they did every day, they'd remember the brave and wonderful father they loved and missed so much.

## Discussion Questions

1. Why was Jean sad when she heard that the war was over?

2. Why are we lucky that Canadians like Jean's father went away to war?

*Jean MacNeil (Airth) pictured above with her little sister Mora, was born in Ottawa, Ontario. In 1941, when her father went overseas, Jean was an 11-year-old schoolgirl.*

# ❧ The Poppy ❧

"**I**n Flanders Fields the poppies blow…" Cameron recited as he listened to the sad sound of the lament being played on the bagpipes. He stood at the edge of the memorial park, huddled next to his little brother Graham and his grandparents. It was a damp, cold November 11th morning.

"I know the whole poem," Cameron continued. "Would you like to hear it?"

Before his grandfather had a chance to answer, Graham whispered proudly, "I know some of that poem too!"

Their grandfather smiled and replied, "Yes, we would like to hear it. You could say it together."

With hushed voices, the boys recited the three verses of John McCrae's famous poem. Graham didn't know all the words, but he joined in whenever he could.

"Well done, boys," their grandfather said when they'd finished. Their grandmother hugged them a little closer, trying to shelter them from the bitter north wind.

"When you learned the poem, did you learn where Flanders Fields are?" their grandfather asked.

The boys shook their heads no, and waited for their grandfather to speak.

"Flanders is part of a country called Belgium. It's one of the many faraway places where Canadians have gone to war to help people."

"Is there still a war there?" Graham asked.

"No," replied their grandfather. "The Belgians have lived in peace for many years, but they are still very grateful to the Canadians who came to their rescue."

"Do they all wear poppies on their jackets like we do?" Cameron asked as he looked down at the bright red flower that was pinned to his collar.

Their grandfather shook his head. "Customs are a little different in every country," he said. "Our Canadian custom of wearing a poppy on Remembrance Day started a long time ago. It started a few years after Colonel John McCrae wrote the poem that you just recited. Wearing a poppy shows that we remember the brave men and women who went away to war and died."

"When I was little," their grandmother added, "my mother pinned a poppy on my coat every Remembrance Day before we went to the ceremony in our little town park. She always said, 'Today we need to have a special thought about your cousin Dick'."

## Remembrance Day November 11th

On the eleventh hour of the eleventh day of the eleventh month in the year 1918, the armistice agreement ending the First World War took effect. The following year, King George V expressed the wish that people throughout the British Empire would pause for two minutes at 11 o'clock on November the 11th to remember those who had died in the war. In Canada, this observance was known as Armistice Day until 1931 when parliament passed a law making the 11th of November a holiday to be known as Remembrance Day.

"Did he die in the war?" Cameron asked.

"Yes," his grandmother answered sadly. "He was a pilot who had a dangerous job flying wounded people to hospitals. Just before the end of the war, when everybody in his hometown was hoping he'd return home safely, they heard the awful news that he'd died."

"Well, I don't remember anyone that went away to war and died," Graham said. "Why do I wear a poppy?"

"Even if we don't know anyone who died in a war or on peacekeeping duty, we wear poppies to remember all of the Canadians who have lost their lives while trying to help others. We must never forget that we live in peace because brave people went to war to make sure there was peace."

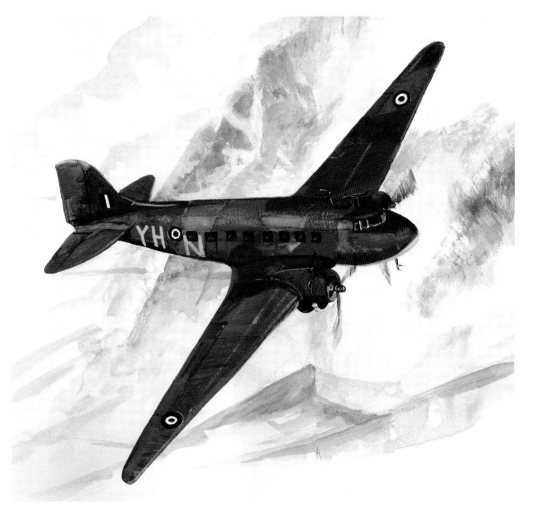

*Flying Officer Clinton Richard (Dick) Ryerse was born in Port Dover, Ontario. Dick joined the Royal Canadian Air Force, qualified as a pilot, and was sent overseas in 1940. On 2 August 1945, the Ryerse family was told that Dick was presumed to have died when the plane he was flying went missing on 19 September 1944. He was 24 years old.*

Cameron and Graham shivered with cold as they stood quietly watching the Remembrance Day ceremony. They watched as the men and women marched past wearing colourful medals. They listened as a trumpeter played the Last Post before a long silence. Graham wanted to ask his grandmother how long he had to wait before he could talk, but she had her eyes closed and he could tell she was thinking. He decided to wait quietly so that he didn't disturb her. When the sound of the trumpet suddenly broke the silence, his grandmother opened her eyes.

"Did you have a special thought about your cousin?" Cameron asked shyly.

His grandmother nodded yes as she looked up at the cold gray monument and the wreaths of poppies that had been placed at its base. "Yes, Cameron. I thought of Dick and I thought of the thousands and thousands of other men and women I never knew, who gave up so much for us."

The little group watched the end of the ceremony before their grandfather said, "Now it's time to leave."

"Is Remembrance Day over?" Graham asked.

As they walked slowly away, their grandfather replied, "Today's ceremony is over, but every single day we should remember why we live in peace and we should be grateful."

## John McCrae

In 1915, a Canadian named John McCrae wrote the poem "In Flanders Fields". Although Colonel John McCrae is best known as a poet, he is also remembered as a brave and caring doctor and soldier who served Canada in two wars.

## Discussion Questions

1. Why do we wear poppies?

2. What does freedom mean?

3. Why should we be grateful to the people who served our country in war?

# In Flanders Fields

In Flanders fields the poppies blow
Between the crosses, row on row,
That mark our place; and in the sky
The larks, still bravely singing, fly
Scarce heard amid the guns below.

We are the Dead. Short days ago
We lived, felt dawn, saw sunset glow,
Loved, and were loved, and now we lie
In Flanders fields.

Take up our quarrel with the foe:
To you from failing hands we throw
The torch; be yours to hold it high.
If ye break faith with us who die
We shall not sleep, though poppies grow
In Flanders fields.

- John McCrae

## Special Thanks

The Poppy, as a symbol of remembrance, is a trademark controlled by The Royal Canadian Legion. The Legion has graciously permitted use of the Poppy symbol in *What We Remember*.

We are grateful to Mrs. Joan Macpherson for permitting the use of "Wait for Me, Daddy", the famous photograph by her father, Claude Dettloff.

# Fact Box Sources

page 6 .........................National Capital Commission website http://www.canadascapital.gc.ca

page 9 .........................G.F.G. Stanley, Canada's Soldiers, MacMillan, Toronto, 1960, p. 313

page 10 .......................ibid, p.328 Aleks Deseyne ed., Passchendaele 1917, Dejonghe, Ieper, 1987

page 14 .......................Granatstein & Morton, A Nation Forged in Fire, Lester & Orpen Dennys, Toronto, 1989, p. 40

page 16 .......................ibid, pp. 36-38

page 20 .......................Carolyn Gossage, Greatcoats and Glamour Boots, The Dundurn Group, Toronto, 2001, p. 199

page 24 .......................Watson & Graham, The Canadians, McArthur & Company, Toronto, 2002, p. 20

page 27 .......................Granatstein & Morton, A Nation Forged in Fire, Lester & Orpen Dennys, Toronto, 1989, p. 81

page 28 .......................Veterans Affairs Canada website http://www.vac-acc.gc.ca/remembers/

page 32 .......................http://www.inglewoodcarecentre.com/history/remembranceday2.htm

page 35 .......................John F Prescott, In Flanders Fields, The Story of John McCrae, The Boston Mills Press, Erin, 1985

# Acknowledgements

I am deeply indebted to the people who have shared my dream of teaching young children about the importance of Remembrance.

My heartfelt thanks must be extended to the principal characters of the stories and their relatives — John and Mora Hassell, Malcolm Airth, Colonel Bill Bawden, Jacqueline Brewster, General John deChastelain, Jock MacNeil, and Barbara (Ryerse) Long — who shared their memories with me and allowed me to share their memories with others.

I am extremely grateful to General Paul Manson for believing in this book, and for his generosity in providing wise counsel from the very beginning.

It is an immense honour to have received enthusiastic support from Lieutenant-Colonel the Honourable Barnett J. Danson. I am touched and humbled by his kindness, his energy, and his unflagging optimism.

I feel very privileged to have received an endorsement from Canada's pre-eminent military historian, Dr. Jack Granatstein. His opinion means everything to me.

For their considerable efforts in helping me with this project, I also want to thank Lieutenant-General Charles Belzile, Brigadier-General Duane Daly, Senator the Honourable Joe Day, Lieutenant-General René Gutknecht, and Cliff Chadderton.

I cherish the letter of support I received from the internationally renowned author, Roch Carrier.

To my editors and reviewers, I am extremely grateful. I cannot thank Stephanie Goodwin enough — she taught me such a great deal. What a difference she made! Thank you to Dr. Kevin Flynn for providing clear, honest insight. Thank you to Shawn Moreau for her perceptive observations regarding children's sensibilities. Special thanks to my talented 'editor-in-chief', Allison Gibson, and the superb editors-at-large — Jane Alden, Eloise Caverson, Philip Gibson, and MaryAnn deChastelain.

A big thank you to Keira and Matthew for patiently posing for the cover illustration on the hottest day of the summer.

Special thanks must be given to Michelle Gagnon who combined special creativity with technical magic to design the original layout.

There wouldn't be a book without Mervyn Finch. How lucky I am to have such a friend.

To my very tolerant and loving husband and family – thank you.

## About the Author

Lesley Airth is a professional educator with a Masters Degree in Education. She is also the mother of three children. As a Canadian living in Europe for nearly a decade, Lesley attended ceremonies and visited many sites where Canadians are honoured. The profound impact of hearing the stories and seeing the tears of those who were liberated, and their liberators – Canadian veterans who returned to re-visit the people and lands where they had fought and their comrades had died – proved indelible. *What We Remember* is the result of Lesley's passion to ensure young Canadians know that the peace and freedom they enjoy today is the legacy of courage and sacrifice.

## About the Illustrator

Mervyn Finch was born in Wolverhampton, England. He developed a passion for painting and artistic creation at an early age. This passion has remained a constant throughout a varied career that included twenty-two years in the British Army. Merv has settled in Canada where he paints, sculpts, writes and dabbles in the world of high tech training.

Other works include:
*Cameron's Capital Adventure*
*Cameron's Colouring and Activity Book*
*A Gift from Graham*

To order more copies of

# What We Remember

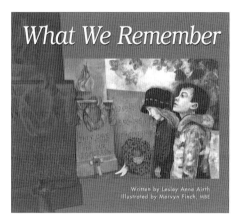

Contact:

**GENERAL STORE PUBLISHING HOUSE**

499 O'Brien Road, Box 415, Renfrew, Ontario  Canada K7V 4A6

Telephone: 1-800-465-6072 • Fax: (613) 432-7184 • **www.gsph.com**

VISA and MASTERCARD accepted.